In the Cot
and
Tim and Bill

Level 2 – Red

Helpful Hints for Reading at Home

The graphemes (written letters) and phonemes (units of sound) used throughout this series are aligned with Letters and Sounds. This offers a consistent approach to learning, whether reading at home or in the classroom.

HERE IS A LIST OF PHONEMES FOR THIS PHASE OF LEARNING. AN EXAMPLE OF THE PRONUNCIATION CAN BE FOUND IN BRACKETS.

Phase 2			
s (sat)	a (cat)	t (tap)	p (tap)
i (pin)	n (net)	m (man)	d (dog)
g (got)	o (sock)	c (cat)	k (kin)
ck (sack)	e (elf)	u (up)	r (rabbit)
h (hut)	b (ball)	f (fish)	ff (off)
l (lip)	ll (ball)	ss (hiss)	

HERE ARE SOME WORDS WHICH YOUR CHILD MAY FIND TRICKY.

Phase 2 Tricky Words			
the	to	I	no
go	into		

TOP TIPS FOR HELPING YOUR CHILD TO READ:

- Allow children time to break down unfamiliar words into units of sound and then encourage children to string these sounds together to create the word.

- Encourage your child to point out any focus phonics when they are used.

- Read through the book more than once to grow confidence.

- Ask simple questions about the text to assess understanding.

- Encourage children to use illustrations as prompts.

This book focuses on /ll/ and /ss/ and is a Red level 2 book band.

In the Cot
and
Tim and Bill

Written by
Georgie Tennant

Illustrated by
Rosie Groom

Can you say this sound and draw it with your finger?

In the Cot

Written by
Georgie Tennant

Illustrated by
Rosie Groom

Dad and Bill. Bill naps. Dad sips.

Bess is a cat. Tess is a dog.

Bess got in but can Tess? No!

Tess is sad. Bess is in the cot.

Dad pops in. Dad nags.

Bess is not in the cot.

Bill naps. Dad sips. Tess pops in.

Tess and Bill sit. Dad pops in.

Dad is mad. Tess is sad.

Bess is in. Tess is in.

A mat is on top of the cot.

Bill naps on a mat. Dad sips.

Can you say this sound and draw it with your finger?

Tim and Bill

Written by
Georgie Tennant

Illustrated by
Rosie Groom

Bess the cat and Tess the dog.

Bill has a cap. It is on Tess!

Tim has a pin. It is in Bess!

Dad pops in. Dad is mad.

Dad has a kit in a tin.

It is a map!

Dad, Bill and Tim dig a pit.

A tin! Tim pops the lid off.

Bill dips in. A kit in a tin!

It can dig and tip. The kids dig.

Dad did the map! Dad did the tin!

Dad did the kit! Dad sits.

©This edition published in 2023. First published in 2021.
BookLife Publishing Ltd.
King's Lynn, Norfolk, PE30 4LS, UK

ISBN 978-1-80155-996-6

All rights reserved. Printed in China.
A catalogue record for this book is available from the British Library.

In the Cot and Tim and Bill
Written by Georgie Tennant
Illustrated by Rosie Groom

FSC
www.fsc.org
MIX
Paper from responsible sources
FSC® C113515

An Introduction to BookLife Readers…

Our Readers have been specifically created in line with the London Institute of Education's approach to book banding and are phonetically decodable and ordered to support each phase of Letters and Sounds.

Each book has been created to provide the best possible reading and learning experience. Our aim is to share our love of books with children, providing both emerging readers and prolific page-turners with beautiful books that are guaranteed to provoke interest and learning, regardless of ability.

BOOK BAND GRADED using the Institute of Education's approach to levelling.

PHONETICALLY DECODABLE supporting each phase of Letters and Sounds.

EXERCISES AND QUESTIONS to offer reinforcement and to ascertain comprehension.

BEAUTIFULLY ILLUSTRATED to inspire and provoke engagement, providing a variety of styles for the reader to enjoy whilst reading through the series.

AUTHOR INSIGHT:
GEORGIE TENNANT

Georgie Tennant is a freelance writer who has written multiple stories for BookLife Publishing. She always knew she would be a writer as she used to present her school teachers with lengthy stories and poems for them to enjoy! Her two sons provide plenty of entertaining material for her writing, which usually appears on her blog or in the local newspaper as the 'Thought for the Week'. When she isn't writing, she is working as a part-time secondary school English teacher, where she has the joy of inspiring slightly bigger children with the joy of reading good stories. She hopes to write good stories for them one day, too.

This book focuses on /ll/ and /ss/ and is a Red level 2 book band.